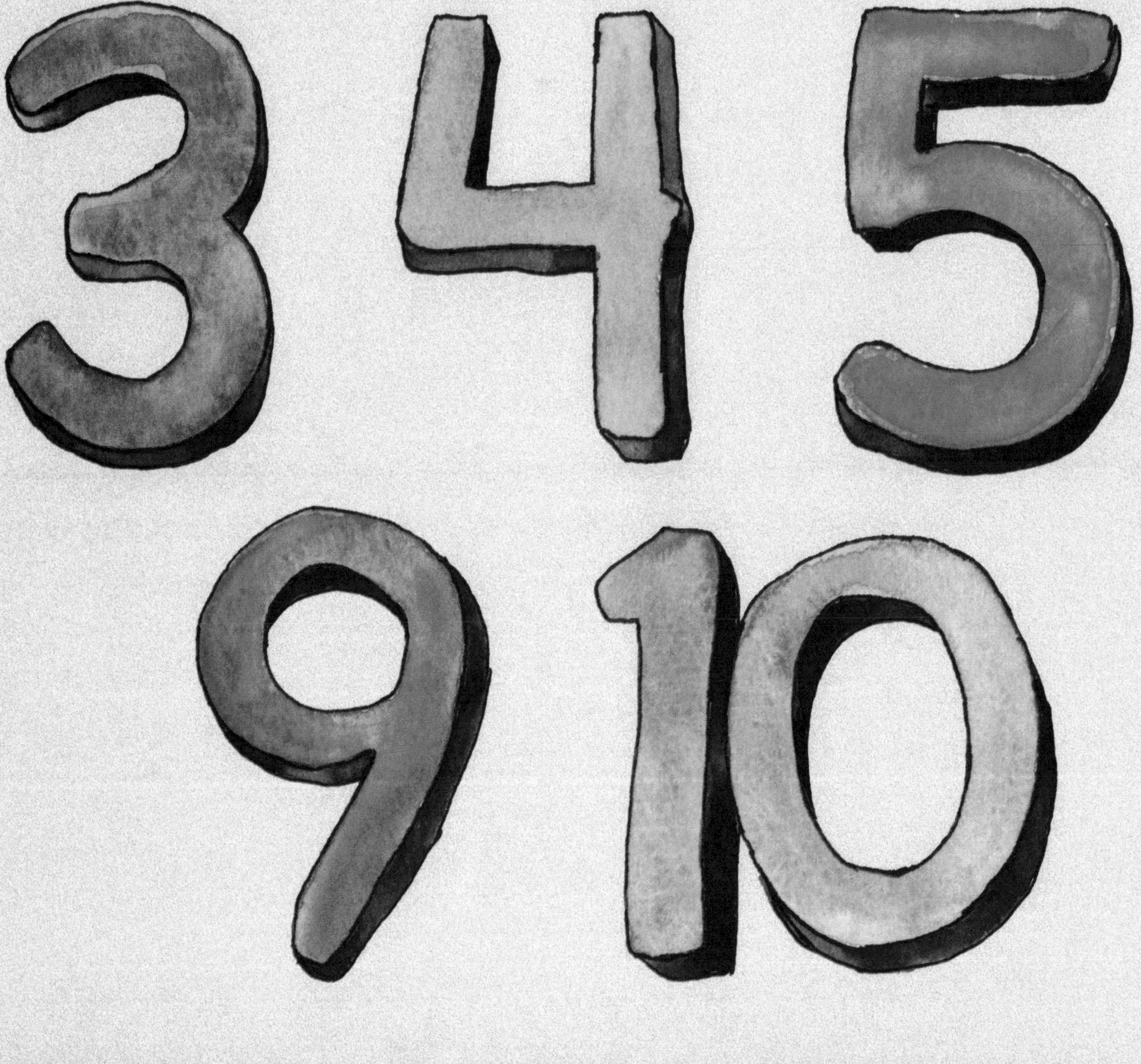
3 4 5
9 10

Published by Scholastic Inc.,
90 Old Sherman Turnpike, Danbury, Connecticut 06816.

SCHOLASTIC and associated logos are trademarks
and/or registered trademarks of Scholastic Inc.

ISBN 0-7172-8609-6

Printed in the U.S.A.

First Scholastic Printing, August 2005

My two Book

by Jane Belk Moncure
illustrated by Kate Flanagan

SCHOLASTIC INC.

New York   Toronto   London   Auckland   Sydney
Mexico City   New Delhi   Hong Kong   Buenos Aires

This is Little **two**.

Little  lives in the house of two.

It has two rooms. Count them. One, two.

Every day Little  puts on her . . .

two shoes

and goes for a walk.

One day, she found
two caterpillars.

Every day the caterpillars changed a little.

Until one day, they grew
into two butterflies.

One.

Two.

How many butterflies flew away?

Little two clapped two claps, can you?

Little 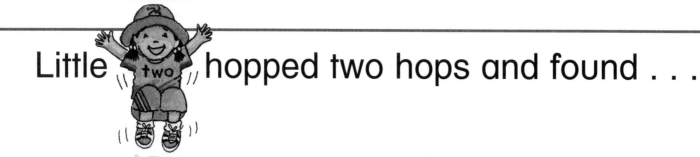 hopped two hops and found . . .

two hens.

The hens said,
Cluck, cluck
two times. Can you?

Then the hens flew away.

Little *two* saw two eggs.

Guess what?

The eggs cracked open.

Out hopped two little chicks.
The chicks said, *Peep, peep*
two times. Can you?

How many baby chicks went hop, hop?

Later, Little  found two lambs.

The lambs were sad. "We are lost," they said.

"We want our mamas!"

Little  two said, "Let's find them.
Come along."

Little two found one . . .

mama sheep.

How many mamas were still missing?

Little two found the other mama sheep.

How many animals
are in the pen?

Next Little  two found . . .

two tadpoles.

She put the two tadpoles in a bowl.

She waited two weeks. Guess what?

The tadpoles grew into frogs.
How many?

Little  two said, "Hop, hop."

The two frogs went hop, hop. Can you?

Then Little two saw . . .

two stars in the sky.

"I must go home," she said.

She yawned two yawns. Can you?

She took off two shoes. One, two.
Then she found . . .

two teddy bears

and two blankets.

Little  **two** hopped—one, two—into bed.

And she went to sleep in two winks.

Little  two found two of everything.

two caterpillars

two lambs

two butterflies

two sheep

two hens

two tadpoles

two frogs

two stars

two eggs

two chicks

two teddy bears

Now you find two things.

"See what I made," said Little 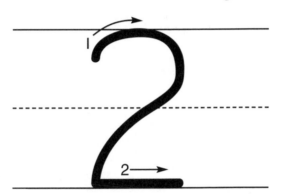.
She makes a 2 this way:

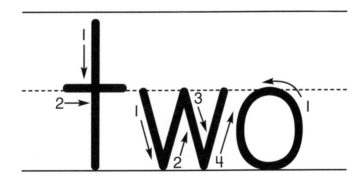

Then she makes the number word like this:

You can make them in the air with your finger.

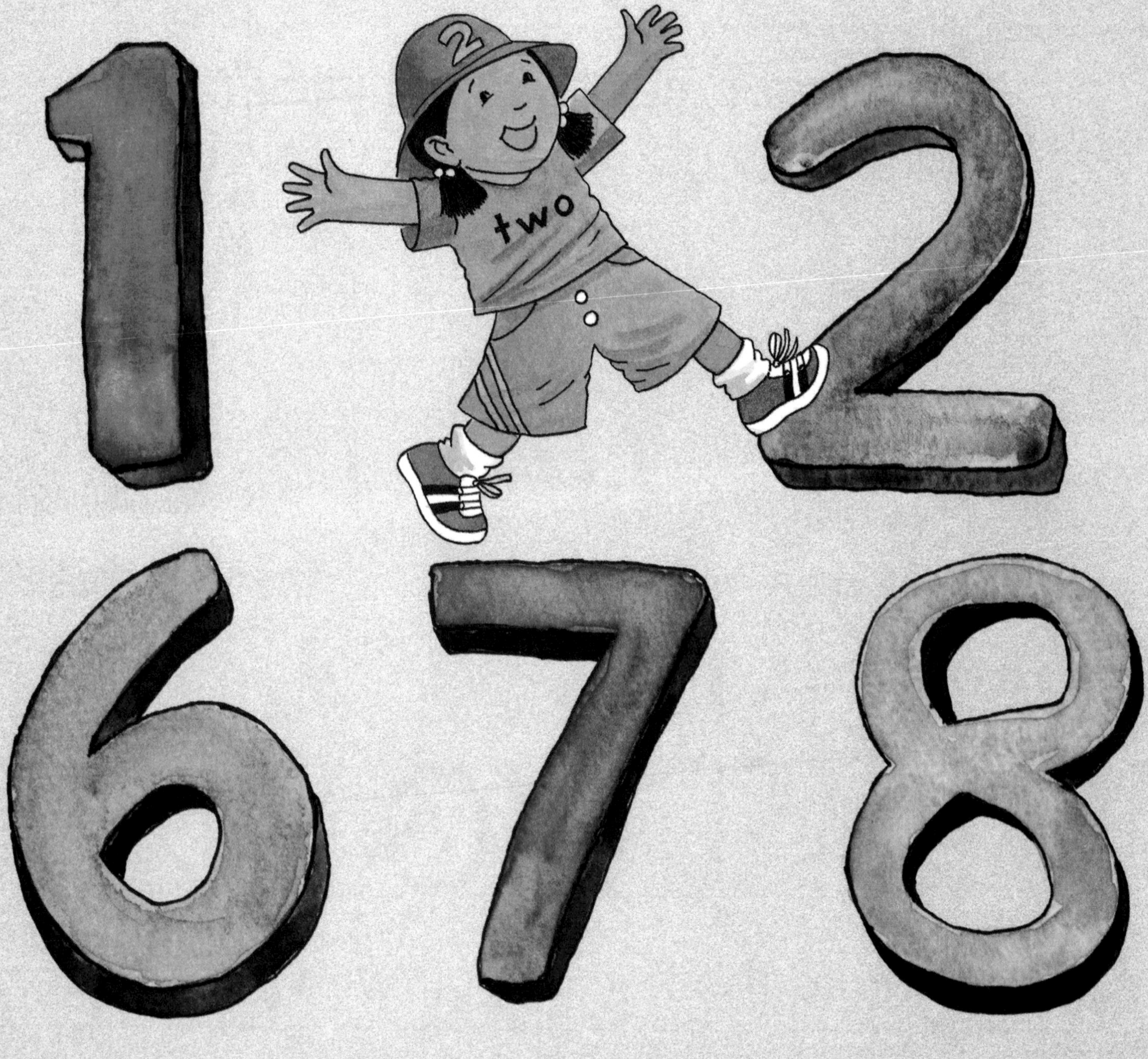
2
two